A BOOK
OF GAMES

Books by Hugh Prather

NOTES TO MYSELF (1970)
I TOUCH THE EARTH, THE EARTH TOUCHES ME (1972)
NOTES ON LOVE AND COURAGE (1977)
THERE IS A PLACE WHERE YOU ARE NOT ALONE (1980)
A BOOK OF GAMES (1981)

A BOOK
OF GAMES

a course in
spiritual play

Hugh Prather

A DOLPHIN BOOK
Doubleday & Company, Inc., Garden City, New York

Library of Congress Cataloging In Publication Data:

Prather, Hugh.
    A book of games.

    (A Dolphin book)
    1. Games.   I. Title.
GV1201.P7   794   80-2840
ISBN 0-385-14779-1

To the children of
The Center for Attitudinal Healing

TO HEAL IS TO MAKE HAPPY
   —A Course in Miracles

INTRODUCTION
by Gerald G. Jampolsky, M.D.*

Hugh Prather once wrote, "There must be another way to go through life besides being pulled through it kicking and screaming." This book is a refreshing guide to that other way. On reading it, it seems natural to me, almost a necessity dictated by consistency, that the pathway to the heart of God be gentle and happy. These games, all of which are very effective mind-training exercises, require no sacrifice or pain. The reader is urged to dance, not plod, his way into a new perception.

The games of the world are legion, and they all have one characteristic in common: the

*Dr. Jampolsky is a psychiatrist and is founder and director of The Center for Attitudinal Healing in Tiburon, California.

results are inevitably distressing, if not tragic. Money, romance, respect, influence, even the games of idleness and isolation, all offer a trophy that begins to tarnish the moment we claim it. In the end, no one is left a winner.

Here are games of a different sort. Each leads to the removal of some block of our awareness of love and thereby promotes our recognition that we are not alone in life. And as these blocks melt in consistent but joyous play, we begin to sense that we already possess what we all desire most deeply: the peace of God.

We learn from this book that our natural state is happiness. We learn that our true and only reality is love, the God Self that joins us together as One Self. And we see that this is meant for today, this instant, as we move from situation to situation, as we encounter people, and make decisions. Happiness is the most practical of tools.

These games come from Hugh's counseling techniques, but more importantly, from his own endeavors to hear and follow the leadings of Love. He is my friend and soul mate, and I am deeply appreciative of these gifts of love to us all.

AUTHOR'S NOTE

A book that contains no attack can be very disconcerting to anyone who is used to looking on attack as an effective means of solving personal problems and the bitter suffering of the world. This book is based on the premise that the nature of the effect will accurately reflect the nature of the means used to produce it. An entirely peaceful approach will produce a wholly peaceful result. This concept is considered naïve, even dangerous, by many. But that will not matter to you if you are willing to merely try the approach suggested. This is a book of **"games"** because it is not essential to your success that you believe the assumptions made. Yet it is all important that you apply the rules of the games as thoroughly and consistently as you can. Nothing more than this is required for you to receive the full benefit of each game. A serious approach to life does not have to be complex and deadly. Quite the contrary. Success is a single idea, simply applied, and joyously felt. The rules of life are fair.

A BOOK
OF GAMES

As you know, there have been rumors of late that a new Master, called by some "the Master of Play," is now traveling the land. It was recently reported that he was engaged in handing out a small book of games. The philosophy it contains is said to be very simple: **Happiness leaves nothing undone.** If you are happy, you cannot fail to hear the Song of God. If you are happy, you have no interest in darkening your mind with grievances against anyone, and so you are naturally kind and consistently fair. And how could you not be free of the world's countless addictions if within you felt a deep con-tentment? You would not pass by anyone in need nor fail to be in the right place at the right time. Can joy and peace ever be out of place? Joy is in the giving of the abundance of joy. And so, by being happy, you are all you ever need be: loving, just, pure, and compassionate. And your every step is guided and blessed by the Song of God.

It is said that as this new Master has traveled about, he has met with surprisingly little resistance. Yet if his teaching is true, then he who is happy is also harmless. And since harm is unthinkable for him, how could he think of being harmed? He simply goes quietly about his work, and yet, it is reported by those who claim to have seen him that his voice and comfort remain with whoever has recognized him.

The little book that the Master gives to anyone who might like to read his teaching is said to contain a single course of study. Perhaps it would be more in keeping with his teaching to describe it as a course of play, since the course itself is nothing more than a series of games. If the one receiving it agrees to play along, the Master himself will create any illusion necessary to set up a game. Often he allows you to believe that you are back in your daily routine, with everything the same, except that now your single purpose for anything you do is to play the game he has assigned you that day.

For example, it is quite possible that you have already met the Master, and he is the one who gave you this book. However, so that you really will believe you are back in your daily routine, he is allowing you to think that you obtained the book under quite different circumstances and that now you are just reading about it. Please do not try to determine which is true, because you may have already agreed to play.

As you begin your course of games, it is very important to remember that whenever you have a question of procedure, no matter how small you consider it, simply pause and ask it of the Master. Be assured that your answer will be in the next quiet thought you have. You may try this right now if you wish. Be still a moment and ask which game is to be the first you will play. You will be told how to select it.

Something may have happened just now that distressed you. Certainly the Master of Play will not allow anyone in his care to remain distressed. He wants you to be happy because the key to his being such a great Master is his recognition that enlightenment and gentleness of thought are exactly the same. Therefore, let us review what may have occurred.

It is possible you heard two answers after you asked. If so, perhaps you wondered which was the Master's voice, and this question may have distressed you. Here is a simple test. One of your thoughts included instructions as to what to do now. That was the Master's voice coming to you as your own thinking. The other thought, if there was one, suggested a reason for you to be anxious, but it offered no clear instructions. In one way or another, the Master always tells you, "Do **this,** for it will please you most," whereas the voice of playlessness counsels conflicting considerations but never points clearly in a direction. Please know that you do not have to spend one moment in fear or conflict. Simply forget what you heard that confused you and follow the voice of peace. Remember also that what you are to do may very well be something you consider to be only mental.

The Master will tell you when you have completed your course of study. He will even tell you whether you need take it at all. In other words, only read as much of this book as makes you happy. Happiness is the voice of the Master. Simply by reading to this point you are now assured that the Master goes with you from this time on.

And so, my fellow playmate, on behalf of the Master of Play, who I, like you, have also met, I wish you a light heart and a gentle vision. Let all your games allow you to sing, and let everything your thought touches turn to music.

TABLE OF GAMES

Secret Agent

A REALITY GAME

Peace is your only purpose now. It is the gift offered you in everything that will occur. Each sight and happening can have no other reason but this.

Whenever you have a moment today, think to yourself a thought like this one: "I will not pause to correct, impress, argue, resist, appease, or oppose. In all my encounters today, let me choose the way of peace."

Today's game can be used in any encounter, chance meeting, or ongoing relationship, whether internal or external. Please elaborate on it in any way that pleases you, but remember to keep clear the purpose of the game.

GAME

You are now a secret agent from a foreign kingdom. The mission your king has personally commissioned to you is as clearly defined as was that of the famous seductresses of the First and Second World Wars whose objectives were to obtain military secrets. To this end, they could say or do anything. Your objective, however, is not to get but only to have. You are to have peace with whomever you encounter. To this end, you can say or do anything. In fact, you are not to be concerned at all with your behavior or with how another acts toward you. Nor are you to distinguish between external encounters and ones that take place only in what you think of as your mind. A recalled encounter or one anticipated or one invented are all equal in importance to "actual" meetings between you and anyone else.

Should someone choose to gossip in your presence or do anything else you might formerly have disapproved of, your instructions are to not denounce him in your mind. Your objective is not to make him conform to judgments of what is "proper" behavior, but only to ensure that there be an actual feeling of harmlessness and gentle caring between you. Likewise, you have no interest in achieving verbal agreement with anyone, knowing that harmony is not held within appearances.

Each time you succeed in allowing even an instant of goodwill between you and another, your duty will be to report this back to your king. This you will do by means of a mental transmitting device which has already been installed. The code phrase you are to use is: "Thank you."

Banker

A PRAYER GAME

Today's prayer game is designed to provide you with an accounting of all your investments. Because your heart is where your treasure is, this accounting is important to you. The Master does not want your heart to ache, and, since pain has nothing to do with progress, there is never any reason why pain need accompany you on your way.

GAME

Three times today, please break with what you are doing for just a moment. For this particular prayer game, it will be helpful if you can interrupt some activity you would ordinarily continue without stopping. It is a mind-set you are being asked to break. Your mind will set a goal that is unimportant, and you will simply remember something of greater importance. For example, while in the "middle" of a meal, you might say to those you are with, "Excuse me. I'll be right back," and then go into a restroom to take a moment to play this game.

During your break, scan your feelings as of that instant. It is not necessary to recall an earlier time when you may have had a stronger feeling. Any feeling you notice now that is not one of pure comfort and joy is sufficient for the purposes of this game. Think of the feelings that fit this description as entries in a savings book or in a current bank statement. Such feelings are an exact accounting of what external appearances you have invested in. You have set a high value on something "out there." Either you want it changed or left unchanged, and you are anxious or sad that this rule of happiness you have made may be broken. The fact that you attempt to set the rules whereby you will be happy should indicate to you that, in a very real sense, your heart is where you have placed your treasure.

Having taken a moment to check the outcomes you have invested in, take one moment more to withdraw your investment, and your heart. Put them where they will not hurt you. Say, "I have no further interest in (what this person decides; how this event turns out; what I need to do to appear 'right'). Instead, I am interested in the peace of God. The peace of God is all I value. The peace of God is all I have, all I am, all I could ever need or want."

Then return to the activity you left, and take with you a single new goal: to be comfortable, to be at ease, to let all things be, and to extend to all the peace of God.

Dancing Band

A WORD GAME

GAME

All words rush to stand in a line, one behind the other, much like the members of a well-trained marching band. When viewed from above, this line is clearly seen to form an arrow. This is equally true of words of thought as it is of the words of conversation.

The arrow that words form points in a direction and asks the one who is being addressed to look within himself and see there what has been indicated. It points either to images of darkness or to a scene of light, to guilt or to holiness and joy.

Which of these you have asked another to direct his attention to can be plainly seen in his reaction. If you try to focus his mind on darkness within him, you have lied and your words will not make him happy. And because you will believe that you have attacked him, even if "for his own good," you will interpret his reaction as an attack on you.

This evidence of vengeance cannot be avoided because you have asked that he be injured, and his apparent injury will point to you as the attacker. Do not now go back and attempt to heal him with your guilt. See only that you have not hurt him because the darkness you pointed to was never there. Can there ever be darkness at the heart of a child of God? And can **you** be guilty if you simply made a mistake?

Turn your words toward reality. Teach only what is actually inside. Reform every thought of condemnation into a celebration of innocence. Let your words play music and your mind dance its way to truth, and you will know night no longer.

Crack of Light

A Light Game

GAME

If you were to walk around the outside of a light-filled house, no matter how tightly the shades had been drawn and the doors shut, you would eventually find a speck of light seeping through some crack or tiny hole. It is the nature of light to find a way out.

What you may not know is that if you call to the spiritual light that you see shining from within another, it will bound through any barrier or shield your judgments may have placed in its way. This is true no matter how small the spark of light you recognize may appear to be.

Look first at the evidence of light you do see, then call directly to its Source. Prove to yourself how gladly light will come when it is called. Say only this to the child of God you look upon:

> I know thee who thou art,
> Thou holy child of Light.
> Come forth, and give me your blessing.

Beauty Aids

A REALITY GAME

Because you are more than a body, you are free. Yet to recognize your freedom, you must give yourself over to a lovely use. When the mind begins to suspect that to give is indeed as happy as to receive, awareness of the body starts to fade. You are intensely aware of your body only when you are mistakenly thinking of it as a device for attaining what you want. A "getting mechanism" is not a pretty concept, and so it follows that when the body is used in this way, the mind will not turn to it to think a lovely thought. Yet the mental state called "feeling ugly" not only looks to the body to get what it wants but also to the body to use and enjoy it. It has now become both the means and the end within the mind's preoccupation with getting more. This is a misuse of the body's natural function which is to permit the mind to extend love in a way that will be recognized and appreciated by others.

The body is like a speaker system or a television screen. It remains neutral until a thought passes through it. If the thought is lovely, then the communication system through which it passes is appreciated. If it isn't, the resulting ugliness is no more the body's than poor programming belongs to the television screen it came through.

Beauty is a thought that extends and thereby sets free. Ugliness is a thought that turns back on itself and so becomes its own jailer. Today's game is designed to practice this simple difference.

GAME

Last night, while you were driving home, one of those big, strange lights that sometimes hovers above single cars traveling down deserted highways, hovered above your car. You were "teleported," a little awed but unharmed, aboard a beautiful spacecraft. There, friendly life-forms offered you apologies and warm drinks. It seems they had selected you for an experiment, and once you heard what they had in mind, you were eager to cooperate.

Into each part of your body that you thought of as lacking, misshapen, or in any way a threat to you, these friendly aliens, without your feeling a thing, located a tiny communicating device which would instantly transmit a mental message to anyone who looked at or even thought of that part of your body. The message that the one who looked at you would always receive was this: "Bless you. Be you comforted."

Now, as you go through this day, you are noticing how your nose, pimple, stomach, deformity, voice, age, hair, or whatever it was about your body you thought was a threat to you, functions only to bring comfort to others. If you are thin or fat, tall or short, you see the twinkle in other people's eyes who are shaped like you, and you find you now have no desire to separate yourself from them by changing your shape. If your right hand is missing a finger, whenever this is felt by the one who reaches to shake your hand, you now see the gentleness in his eyes, and you know that he is assured that, like you, he too has nothing to fear from his body.

You were surprised last night that the aliens also planted communicating devices in the features of your body that you were proud of. You had not realized that you also thought fearfully about these parts. Yet now you recognize that instead of trying to use these physical characteristics to produce a feeling of need, longing, or deprivation in others, it delights you much more to know that there is nothing about you that does not offer rest and assurance to others.

The aliens told you that the experiment was

for one day, at the end of which you would receive a gift of thanks for your cooperation. The gift was that, whenever you wished, you would be able to use your body in this new way even after the communicating devices were removed. They said that all you would have to do is change the direction of your thoughts. Instead of letting them boomerang back to form your self-image, you need only allow them to flow gently outward to others. This, they said, you would be able to do by recalling the words, "Bless you. Be you comforted."

In the past, your self-image was formed by what you believed others thought of you. The essential question you asked about any aspect of your body was, "What thought will the person who looks at me hold in his mind?" And you viewed your body through what you imagined the contents of his mind to be. Rarely did you ask, "What thought do I keep in my mind?" because you did not believe that this question related to how lovely you felt. But you **are** lovely, and your attempts to second-guess what others think and your efforts to change their minds only cause you to doubt yourself. Do not believe you must constantly tinker with your body, its appearance, its standing, or its health, in order to change what you think you are. You will know the beauty of simple giving when you no longer allow your thoughts to curve back at you. To think gentle thoughts about yourself, you need only think gently.

Perhaps it is now that you recall the aliens' marvelous and widely varying shapes. As is yours, how rich a planet is theirs, with so many different kinds of bodies to let their eyes dance upon.

Invisible Faucets

A LIGHT GAME

GAME

Between your temple and your ear, one on each side of your head, you will find the handle of a faucet. These can be felt but cannot be seen. They are light faucets installed by the Master. You can use them anytime you wish. Simply reach up with both hands and turn them on, and light will sweep through your mind and throughout every part of your body. It will fill each cell to brimming until all of them shimmer with brilliance. The pores of your body will overflow with light, and you will seem to dance like a rainbow on the sea.

Mist

A PRAYER GAME

GAME

Today's prayer game can be done anytime and as often as you wish. The only caution is that you should be aware that your ego may react with sadness to the first step, even though the interpretation on which that rests is completely inaccurate. If you should notice this reaction, it will probably give you a fuller, happier, more accurate sense of the game to include all three steps each time you play.

The world you see can be compared to a mist rising in front of a vast and magnificent scene of beauty. While watching the mist, one is likely to imagine that he sees shapes of all kinds: moving bodies, plants, buildings, and whole sequences of events. Yet what he sees is really no more than the random swirls of the mist itself.

However, the beauty behind the mist can still be dimly seen. At first it will appear to shine from out of the very mist figures themselves. It should therefore be remembered that two things are always being seen: the mist and the beauty. Yet they are entirely separate even though they appear to combine within the same form.

This prayer game will allow the mist to

clear a little so that you may see the source of beauty more clearly. You are like a sleeping child being held in its parent's arms. You are still misty with sleep, but, even now, you are beginning to feel the arms of love that encircle you.

Step One: Take note of everything you are aware of. Notice all your sensations: the pressure of the chair against your body, the feel of your clothes. Become aware of the various objects around you. Notice sounds and smells. Take note of any memories or anticipations, thoughts of any type. Exclude nothing at all. Then think first along the following lines:

"All of this will be forgotten. (This chair is exactly like that sound; it will be forgotten. The sensation of this cloth is in no way different from the light reflecting off that glass; it will be forgotten. The scene I just remembered is like that body; it will be forgotten.) Each thing I am aware of now, in time will be forgotten. And none of it will ever be remembered again."

Step Two: Now follow with this thought: "Everything I see holds limitless value.

(That plant is the same as that power line; the value it contains is without end. This feeling of warmth is like that sky; its worth cannot be measured. This sound of breathing does not differ from this image of expectation; it holds unlimited beauty.) The worth in each sensation, each idea, every emotion is immeasurable.

Step Three: Even though the exact words are not important, please finish with this idea, because it is a full acknowledgment of the Beauty just in back of the mist. And that Beauty is your Home and your Self.

I am in an ocean of Beauty.
I am in a sea of God.
I hear nothing but a Song of Love.
I see nothing but limitless Splendor.
And all I feel is eternal Peace.

Courtroom

A REASONING GAME

Prosecuting and defending are the same. In fact, each one relies on the other for meaning. If your mind assumes a defensive posture, you thereby make your attacker. If you "see" an enemy, you split your mind. Safety lies in wholeness and acceptance and in the awareness of oneness. Gentleness of thought responds to violence with healing, for it recognizes that anger in any form is a call for help. There is nothing practical in assuming that reality must be guarded against. If it would indeed be helpful for you to avoid a particular experience, God will direct you very specifically in this. Correcting another is not a "favor" to him or to yourself. Do not allow your mind to continue to question, confront, or disagree, for if you assume error or guilt in another, you will not be in a mental position to accept the blessing being offered you. Instead, answer every call for help with help, every question of innocence with an inner smile and nod. You are a healer, not a destroyer, and you make no judgments concerning the form in which your love and understanding is requested.

GAME

Today you are in the legal profession, and you have an unheard of speciality: forensic healing. This new profession will allow you to practice actual law and forget the "laws" of illusion. Illusions cannot have the force of law, but they will appear to as long as they are believed. What is not often recognized is that the mind must remain very active in order to sustain a belief in what is not there. In other words, it must prosecute. Rest from such activity **is** healing. Nothing more than mental rest is needed.

The courtroom in which you are to practice is, as usual, your daily life. Today you are free to hold two "legal" positions and one that is "illegal." The "illegal" position is that of prosecuting attorney. This position will only be offered to you today by your ego. The two legal positions are that of advocating attorney and judge. To assure that as judge you will be incorruptible, you will not be asked to pass judgment but only to exercise one of two functions: you may declare a recess or you may dismiss the case. Here, then, is how the game is played:

Your ego will "hand" you a case to try. It is

relatively easy to recognize when this has occurred because it will involve your having to follow up by "thinking about" the evidence of someone's guilt. It is not possible to occupy your mind with anything other than this instant without starting to build a case against something. Love can show you the past or future, but this will always be marked by joy and will illumine the present at the same instant. In all other instances, any turning over in the mind of what is now through or any anticipating of what has not yet occurred is ego-motivated. And the ego's purpose is to sort out evidence that will "prove" someone wrong.

Whenever you have allowed your mind to become engaged in this unhappy pursuit, you have assumed the "illegal" role of prosecuting attorney. When you become aware of this, you have the opportunity to choose instead one of the alternative roles. At the start, it might be easier to take the role of advocate and then follow this with the role of judge. As advocating attorney you can point out to your mind any or all of the following facts:

1. Change takes place only in the present.
2. To continue rewriting the past or future

is impractical because it does not call for a decision **now.**

3. In order for past guilt or future danger to be argued at all, the mind must act arbitrarily in selecting certain scenes for evidence and disregarding any that would refute the argument.

4. This mental activity does not make you happy or safe and so does not allow you to be open to those around you.

5. You do not want what thinking about the past or future has to offer you.

Now you are ready to assume the role of judge. As judge you can forget the grievance temporarily or you can dismiss it eternally. If you discover that you have not chosen final dismissal, remember that by repeatedly stepping away from this type of mental activity whenever you recognize it, that is, by calling a recess each time that it begins, your consistency will soon have the force of one eternal decision. This effect will follow naturally from the fact that you have chosen to be vigilant. Very soon, your ego will stop even the attempt to hand you this particular case for your consideration. And with each stand you take, refusing one after another all further cases, the overall force of all ego offerings will diminish, and your consequent gain in freedom will be enormous.

Names

A WORD GAME

Names, terms, categories, and other designations are used by your ego to maintain in you a sense of isolation. This is only one of thousands of "proofs" it has for separation. Your ego reasons that since "your" name is different than the names you give to others, you must be separate from them. Assuming this is true, it follows that what you think does not affect them, and you remain unchanged by their feelings and thoughts. This is not a happy way to look at life. It results in loneliness, depression, and a sense of in-significance concerning whatever you think and do, all of which is actually unfounded. You can safely dismiss all evidence given to you by your ego in support of division and separation, and today's game will help you see that you do in fact have this freedom of choice.

GAME

Today, replace all names with only one. Whatever you see or think of, give it gladly your single name. You may use a word that you already understand and love, or you may choose one from these: God. Love. Light. I. One. Peace. Please do not neglect to include yourself in all you name as one with you.

Mind Projector

A REALITY GAME

Today, a single principle of change will be practiced. It is this: "How I want the world to be is the sole determiner of how I will think it is. Today I wish everything well."

The content of all thought and therefore of all situations is one of two states: peace or conflict, comfort or anxiety, gentleness or attack. The content is entirely subject to your will, but external circumstances, if dealt with separately, cannot be controlled. What you "like" in any situation is its content and not its form. And you alone determine content. But the content will not change as long as you use your mind to attack the outward form.

Since every thought you think appears in some external form within your experience, today's game is designed to make this cause and effect relationship more obvious. Briefly stated, the rule is that form follows content, therefore only content need ever be considered.

GAME

The Master has invented a "mind projector," and, knowing that you could possibly be influenced by the widely held belief that minds are located inside heads, he has installed it at the center of your forehead. If you will reach up now and feel just one inch above the bridge of your nose, you will see for yourself what an excellent job he did in disguising it as just another paper-thin layer of your skin.

Naturally, this projector is thought-activated. Simply wish it on rather than turn it on. By playing with it for a moment, you will notice it has two features: a light signal and a corrector switch.

1. The light signal reveals the inner nature of the flow of external events. Instead of having to rely on old positions such as "I don't like to eat squash" or "I like to read mysteries," by using this feature you will no longer have to decide beforehand about anything, nor will you have to judge something, or someone, by what its appearance reminds you of. In fact, any pre-judging on your part will probably prevent you from noticing the projector's quiet evaluation of the inner tone of the situation you are in. This tone or inner quality will be

signaled to you in the following way: A continuous and gently expanding light will mean that the content is wholly love. Flashes of light and darkness in which the degree of light steadily declines will be your sign that the inner tone of the situation is conflicted and fear dominated. The mind projector will cast one of these two light signals on everything you see, so that even though the change may at first seem subtle, it will be unmistakable if you are looking for it.

2. If you don't like the content of your present circumstances, by activating the corrector switch you can change it to a content you will enjoy and yet leave the appearance of things unmanipulated. "Un-manipulated" means you feel free for outward appearances to change naturally without your having any preference or even interest in their course. You will know if you have activated the switch when you can sense quite clearly that everyone around you is also comfortable and happy. However, if you still believe there is an advantage, or even a slight benefit, to you for anyone else to continue experiencing the content of the situation as afflicting, the mind projector will honor your wish and not

permit the switch to be activated. Merely wish the corrector switch "on" and immediately the content of your thought, and therefore the content of the outward situation, will turn from fear to love, from conflict to comfort. But remember, please, you must wish it activated for everyone in the situation.

Thoughts set the goal and therefore start the traveler on his way. Thoughts make the pathway smooth or rough and determine the time of arrival. Every thought is but a step in some direction and a destination reached through pain or peace. Thoughts include consequences, and their results are immediate. It is **this** thought, and not the one before, that is the practical object of attention, yet the direction of the stream of thought remains unchanged until a new goal is set.

Friends and Strangers

A WORD GAME

How much of the world do you react to and how much do you see? Whatever you react to is from your past and is not in the present situation. Therefore, you do not see it, you only remember it. Whatever you react to, you are controlled by, and to be controlled by anything is not to be free. To react to everything is to be in pain continually. To love is to free all you see from how you remember it. Now and love are the same.

GAME

You are going to do something for your friends today that they will love. You are going to see them as strangers. Nor will strangers themselves be left out of your kindness, for they will become old friends. Simply see every friend as a stranger and every stranger as a friend.

Pretend that you have heard that this friend has undergone a complete personality transplant. Or pretend that he has been possessed by an angel. He looks familiar, but don't you be fooled. See how many new things you can recognize about him. Just click them off in your mind and notice your delight at each new discovery. For, remember, he is totally different within. This is a game, but what you are seeing is not self-delusion.

And with each stranger you meet today, say to yourself, "There walks my lifelong friend. I know everything there is to know about him." Remember his birth, his childhood, the pains and disappointments he has had, and also the momentary highs and cresting victories. And then recall that underlying all these turnings of fate has been the steady emergence of his lovely Self, a Mind precisely like your own. This stranger has indeed gone through everything you have. You do in fact know him. All that is true of you is true of him. You can love him without hesitation.

By exercising your ability to remember this instant, you will see clearly that all that is real is now, and all that is now is new, and all that is new is forever and forever.

Miracle Wand

A Light Game

GAME

On your hip, held there with a thin golden chain, the Master has placed a miracle wand. It looks very much like the once widely used magic wand except that nothing about it is in any way mysterious, illogical, or "magical." As you might expect, it has several attractive features. The special rainbow feature is the one you will be using today. All other features you will easily discover the next time you play with the wand.

Can you imagine how happy its bright yellow belt makes a bumblebee feel? Or how delighted a daffodil is with its soft-suede yellow jacket? And the sky truly grins with primrose-colored clouds as the sun rises to greet it. For a moment, it looks like the smile ·of a halloween pumpkin with a twinkling yellow candle held in its mouth. Pull your miracle wand out from under its chain of gold and touch lightly each of these sparks of yellow light, and the many, many others that you see, and then tap once the one you wish to bless. All the golden light you have gathered will flash in his features and sweep throughout his hands and limbs, and he will sparkle like a freshly lit fire in a hearth. Now he knows the joy of bumblebees, the gentleness of daffodils, and the splendor of the rising sun.

Again, look over this lovely earth. Do you see the purple robe that drapes the king? Soft it is where it brushes his neck and wrists. And do you see how peacefully the blueberries sleep in the purple shadows of the forest? No queen, sleeping on blue velvet, has had a deeper rest than this. And no tiny robin, snug in its blue-tinted egg, could ever be safer. So run your wand along the soft skin of mulberries and touch the turquoise troughs between the ocean's waves. Gather in the light of plums and forget-me-nots, lapis lazuli and lavender mountains in the dawn. Now turn to this one you touched with yellow and touch him now with blue. See the peace of a still blue sky in every part of him. See his smile open like the opening blue fan of a peacock's tail. And let his eyes dance like sapphires.

Follow now with green, and the orange of apricots, and the red of roses. And when you have brought all the colors of the rainbow to this one you bless, combine them all into a single burst of pure white light. And let this blessed one be brilliant, a shining sun forever set in the shining heavens.

Dreamer

A REALITY GAME

There is no problem that a quiet mind will not answer, because all problems arise from intense mental activity. Stillness permits a gentle correction of perception to occur. To see any light at all is to no longer see darkness. Any aspect of happiness, when chosen over mental pressure, will bring with it all happiness. And if one is happy, he is also kind.

In order to sustain a still mind, it is helpful to recognize what disturbs it. Your ego is a mental premise that you are only part of what you see, that you are one body among many. If this were true, it would indeed follow that everything else you see is potentially a threat. What was in your interest would not be fully in the interest of any other living thing, even though the conflict in interests might at times seem so mild as to almost disappear. Whenever you believe it will benefit you to identify with your ego, you throw your mind into opposition with everything else it experiences. This, of course, shatters your mental peace, and you are no longer happy or kind.

Why, then, would anyone choose to identify with his ego? Because the premise has already been accepted. If you are nothing but a body, then you are lacking. And if a lack exists, it is reasonable to fill it. If you believe you are alone and very small, the only place to get what you lack is from what is not you. And if what is not you refuses to cooperate, as it always does to some extent, then you find yourself at war. That is why no external struggle ever succeeds. The premise, that you are separate, has not been questioned. Stillness automatically questions and rejects that premise. You cannot be still without recognizing that you are all of what you see, and so you do in fact wish everything well.

How can stillness allow this change of perception? Because what is real is also obvious. If the mind is busy, it is attempting to overlook the obvious. There is no need to search. There is no need to ask, "What am I?" Nothing needs to be answered because there is no question about what is. Stillness allows you to see what is, which you cannot do when you are mentally striving, searching, con- fronting, taking, warring. It is safe to be happy. It is practical to trust. It is intelligent to love. It is not only dignified and honorable—it is glorious to be kind.

If you wish, today you may rule the world. Everyone, every event, everything will be subject to your will. To do this, only one thing is required of you: harmlessness, total and complete.

How does one attain such a powerful state? He need only refuse to be deceived any longer. What if you were already in control of everything? What if nothing, including the world, was outside your will? What if everything had always been up to you, and you had only forgotten this fact? Remembering it would then restore full power to you. You would not need to do anything to anyone in order to get it. No external intervention would be required. You would simply say, "I remember now; I am in control. How, then, do I want everything to be?"

In order to control something, it is not necessary to believe it is under your control, if you are willing to act as though it were. If someone made a barbell out of paper and asked you to try to lift it, even if you didn't believe you could pick up something that looked so heavy, if you were willing to try, you would lift it quite easily. Today's game is really a game of willingness. You are asked to be willing to remember one thought, and that thought only, throughout the day. You are not asked to believe it, but only to think as if you believed it. Thinking as if is something one frequently does in fantasies. Although he does not necessarily believe the premise, he allows himself to think what would follow from the premise if it were true. And this is actually what most of the games in this book request that you do. Today's premise, however, may seem frightening to your ego because it knows that if you were to accept the idea fully, you would have no further use for an ego. Here, then, is the game.

GAME

Today, remember this one thought: When you "woke" this morning, you did not wake at all, you only passed from one dream to another. This day, then, is still your dream. You are not now a lonely figure any more than the solitary body that was the focus of your attention was your actual identity in your dream last night. You were all the figures you saw because the entire dream was yours alone. Since everything that occurs is in your mind, you naturally wish for your mind a happy dream. And what you wish for your mind is what you wish for the dream world in which you live. As a dreamer, you cannot be happy unless the contents of your mind are happy. Therefore, wish the whole to be at peace. Suffer not at all one unforgiving thought.

Say to yourself, "Today, I am the dreamer of this dream. Everything is therefore as I wish it to be. How, then, do I wish it?" And now bless everyone you see, and everything. Today, no darkness is outside your reach, because nothing is outside of you today. You live the contents of your mind today, and only that. Today, there are no other minds.

So be still a moment, and forgive each thing within your mind. You wish a dream of love in which to move about, not a dream of angry judgments and of hate. Today, an entirely different goal is yours: You rule the world. And you will the world into a kingdom of light.

Reflecting Pool

A PRAYER GAME

To experience peace it is only necessary to practice the condition that will allow peace to come to your awareness. Peace is a given. It is the very fabric of your mind. You can look away from it and think you have lost it, but you can no more destroy it than you can destroy yourself. Peace returns whenever you rest from defending yourself against it.

The condition which permits peace to enter your thought is very simple: no war. Mentally step away from confrontation whenever you sense that your mind has become engaged in it. Into a clear space, a still spot of rest, peace will gladly enter.

GAME

Think of your mind as a circular pond or reflecting pool into which God shines continually. In order to have the bright, still peace of God deep within you, it is only necessary that you wipe from your mind all the ripples of agitation, all the disturbed patches of resentment and longing and fear. Allow no dark images of any kind to cloud the crystal purity of your thought. Your quiet attention will calm the contents of your mind if you will allow it to move gently about. Its natural function is to purify. Only the fixed and hard focus of your attention can cost you your peace, because light will of itself extend and clarify. Today, practice having a mind that is a still mirror of clarity, a perfect surface into which God can smile.

Facts

AN OBSERVATION GAME

GAME

To truly see a fact is to identify the grounds for your peace and safety. It is to know why you can rest in trust. Real facts are a comfort. If the thought or thing you are looking at makes you sad, some interpretation is being made that is not correct. Whenever you see what is actually taking place, on any level of description, you cannot remain unhappy for long. Today, be as factual as you can, and the day will indeed be a good one. Say of all things, "Let me see this exactly as it is. Let me not distort it by judging it."

Here are a few examples of easy-to-see facts:

Facts about money: 1. Money is little pieces of paper and round metal discs. That is hardly anything to be afraid of or to use for self-esteem. 2. Money buys things, but things represent experiences. What you want is always an experience. Money is not the **only** way to have it. 3. You are given what you need to do the work you are here to do.

Facts about relationships: 1. Feeling close to or distant from someone are not feelings that come from the proximity of that person's body. 2. To try to force someone to be physically near you or to "communicate" with you is to oppose his will. And to oppose another's will is to **seek** to separate yourself from him. 3. Whoever comes, God has sent. And God will send you whomever you need the instant you truly need him.

Facts about desires: 1. Body-oriented desires are only misinterpretations of your deep yearning for the Love that you already are. That is why you need not fear them or fight them. 2. To hide anything is to keep it. And tight is the grip of guilt. 3. When you no longer believe that you have something to fear from showing your desires to God, He will take them and reinterpret them in a way that will bless and bless and bless you and will never hurt you or anyone else again.

Questions

A REASONING GAME

GAME

Every question tells the questioner where to begin. Every question takes a certain description of reality for granted. Every question makes a statement that is either true or false. Notice what the following questions ask you to believe: Why is there an ego? When did it begin? When will I be free of it?

There are really only two questions. Questions that have no answer are all the same. They request only that you become uncertain and conflicted. All other questions arrive at a single answer and ask you to accept relief.

Today you will ask real questions. Do not strive to answer them yourself; simply allow the answer to be yours. Real questions answer themselves and make you happy. It is therefore good to ask them as often as you wish. Please choose one or two from the following list.

If this is a dream, where am I?

If God is my goal, how will this turn out?

If there is no time, what is there to do?

If God is our Source, who, then, is my enemy?

If God goes with me, how do I feel?

Beachcomber

A LIGHT GAME

There is no place where Love is not. But do you believe this now? To see Love, it is not necessary to construct a belief that you can. Love is not a product of beliefs, and there is already a part of your mind that knows this. But it is necessary to let go, at least temporarily, of your conviction that there is now some place where you cannot see the totally harmless. If you believe it is possible for Love to be excluded from one area of your life, the fear you would have if this "law" were violated constitutes a desire that it not be violated. Therefore it will not be, because Love will never move against your will. Today you are to practice, not trying to make God appear, but allowing vision to **be** by stepping away from the mental blocks you have placed in its way. Every time you have a quiet moment to give, say to yourself a thought similar to this: "I will never see Love where I do not want it to be. Today I will forget all my dark expectations and be glad for every sign of Light no matter where I may find it. Because I seek nothing else, I will find God today."

If you have ever hunted for arrowheads, pottery shards, precious stones, or even coins in a gutter, you know how selective your vision can be. Your mind, when it has a single purpose, can block out everything except the evidence that pertains to only one object. If you are looking for aluminum cans on the side of the road, you will be quite blind to the various types of plants growing there, and vice versa.

Your ability to focus has much farther reaching effects than you may realize, because your mind is literally joined to all other minds. And, equally important, there is never an instant when you are not using this ability in some way. The question, then, is not whether you wish to select your experience but, rather, what experiences you want to have.

GAME

Today you are something similar to a beachcomber. You are a "lightcomber." You are to look for light, and only for light, no matter what name it may come under. Here are a few names by which light is sometimes identified: gentleness, innocence, goodwill, lightheartedness, kindliness, joy. For one day, you are not interested in guilt, grievances, conflict, fear, or judgments. You do not attack the evidences of darkness. To do that is to collect darkness. You will merely overlook them as you would overlook seaweed if your purpose was to find shells. Because today, your only interest is in seeing beauty.

To this end the Master has performed a miracle on your body. He has made your heart a light pouch. It will open at just the touch of a thought, if the thought that touches it contains light. Each time you see even the slightest glimmer of grace, just brush off any shadows that may still cling to it and place this shining piece of God into your heart. If you practice well, a moment may come sometime during the day when it will seem that all things on the earth glow softly.

Time-Savers

AN OBSERVATION GAME

Please add to today's observation game as you wish. The rules will be explained, and certain examples in the form of experiments will be suggested, and, after that, other ways to apply the rules may occur to you. If that does not happen, it will not matter, because the experiments listed will be more than enough to ensure you a full play period.

One way that you sometimes make yourself unhappy is by thinking that the future is up to you. Your ego, believing that there are many directions in which you could walk, reasons that these must be anticipated and judged and one of them selected. Thinking that this mental procedure is always followed, your ego concludes that whatever you ended up doing was what you decided to do beforehand.

This assumption, that your actions follow your plans, leads inevitably to feelings of guilt over what you have done and anxiety over what you will do next. And all of that need not be.

As in its other beliefs, your ego is mistaken about what is occurring. You never decide beforehand because there **is** no beforehand. You always decide now because now is what time it is. Planning is only the ego's decision to be anxious **now.**

Decisions are continuous. They are not occasional bursts of energy that propel you in a certain direction and then must be repeated before you will move again. Cause and effect are simultaneous, and all decisions are "spur-of-the-moment." That is why it is never practical to "think ahead," unless it is to set your overall purpose.

This way of looking at time is frightening to your ego, which refuses to question its assumption that planning determines what you do. If you need to make an appointment, you will make it **now.** Planning to make it does not do anything. Every step you may think is needed for you to take a trip—making reservations, buying tickets, packing bags, and so forth—if they really would be helpful, and helpful in that form, will occur when they occur. You will remember what is in your best interests to remember and forget what is in your best interests to forget, although what your ego judges would "look right" may not happen in that form. Remembering is not a function of anxiety. Forgetting is a decision made this instant. You will not be protected, and your way will not be made easier, by worrying about what to do.

Even if judgment and worry, which are

what planning is, could determine the future, they are based on another equally absurd assumption: that you are more intelligent now than you will be when the time comes for the decision to be made. Even your ego will admit that this is a fallacy, when it observes, time and again, that you are not doing what you "decided" beforehand. As it watches you "change your mind," it will concede that you are better informed than you were and must therefore decide again. It will either assign this interpretation to your actions, or it will tell you that you are crazy.

Please know that all of this confusion need not be yours. If you will trust the present, you can safely neglect the future. The following little experiments will show you that **you** decide all things now, and your ego decides nothing in advance. In fact, your ego must wait for something to happen and then look back and assign a shabby motive. This is the actual attraction of guilt. Your ego can use the feeling of guilt as "proof" that it, and not your Self, was the motivator of what occurred. And that is why all looking back will never teach you anything you can use.

GAME

Allow this thought to accompany each of the experiments you do:

I live in this instant only. There
will never be a time when it is not now.

Experiment: While you are talking to someone today, **mentally** pause in the middle of a sentence and ask yourself if you know how the sentence is going to end.

Experiment: The next time you find yourself fantasizing about the outcome of an unresolved situation, begin mentally listing some of the ways you would "like" for it to turn out. After you have thought of a fair number of these, notice how many of them indicate opposing wishes. Does your ego really know what it wants?

Experiment: You will need a food timer or an alarm clock for this experiment. In as much detail as you can, describe to yourself exactly what you will be doing in five minutes. Include your mood as well as your actions. Then set the alarm and go about your day as usual.

Experiment: The next several mornings when you wake, observe when you "decide" to get out of bed and then observe when you in fact do get out of bed. You will see that there will be unpredictable variations in the time that passes between your "decision" to get up and your action. Sometimes you will act almost immediately; sometimes it will be several minutes or even longer before you arise; other times you will simply find yourself up and will not remember "deciding" at all. Your ego is having to guess at when you will get up.

All of the above experiments—and you may think of others to try—indicate one very freeing fact: your life is not in advance of you. You are not pushing a cart; you are riding one. This means that you may not only trust your life as a whole, you may also trust every instant of it. It really **is** safe to be happy now.

House of Mirrors

A REALITY GAME

Probably you can remember a time when you stood in a mirrored dressing room or between two plate-glass store windows and noticed that with a reflecting surface behind you, the reflecting surface in front of you duplicated your image over and over, each time making it seem smaller and farther away. Mirrors can create the illusion that there are many of you, and each "you" is a different size, with distance or space between all.

In psychology a similar phenomenon is called "projection." Here, however, what is seen is recognized as occurring entirely within the mind. One "projects" his thoughts, feelings, opinions onto another and believes they belong to the other and not to him. One of the more obvious instances of this occurs when one person verbally criticizes another.

Think of someone you have known long and well, and ask yourself what type of behavior in others does he denounce most often. He of course criticizes what he suspects is a fault in himself. And why doesn't he recognize something so apparent? Because he has altered the form of his "fault" just enough to be able to deceive himself that its content is different from what he sees in others. For example, he may think it is a fault he has had but has no longer or one he longs to have but refuses to act out.

Jesus' statement, "Whosoever looketh on a woman to lust after her hath committed adultery in his heart," is thought by many to be unreasonable or "hard." To the contrary, it actually points to the quick and easy way for change to occur. You cannot free your mind simply by changing your behavior. In fact, devoting attention to behavior alone assures that there will be no change of thought. Yet if you are a mind, then in changing your mind you change everything.

Are you a body or a mind? If you are only a body, behavior means everything and thought means very little indeed. But who, having lost one limb or two or all or even more of his body than this, is any less himself than before? Is there any limit to the blessing he can bestow? Does God know him any less?

What you see in others is yourself. Do not be fooled today by your ego's use of mirrors. What you see in the weather will not be the weather's "mood" but yours. Your job, your government, your family will only mirror the motives you believe you yourself are capable of. The conversation you just overheard that you thought was about someone else was about you alone. Did it reflect how fallible you believe you are, or did you hear of the grandeur and beauty of life? Those same words could have been interpreted into a thousand conflicting meanings, and a thousand different egos would have done precisely that. But did you hear the truth? Pause now and listen once again. You have nothing to lose but a shabby self-image.

You are not small and suspect. But the first place you will see your magnificence is in the many mirrors that surround you. Do not be deceived by the outer ring of images, the second- and third-party conversations, the books and magazines, the news broadcasts, and the countless floating rumors. Own them all. They only pass before your eyes to bless you.

How can you change if you do not see and hear exactly what it is you no longer have any use for? Every time you dissociate yourself from the images of your mind that you see in another's eyes, you lose a bright and joyous chance to step into light. Today make all the mirrors sing your praise. Know no other person or thing without love.

GAME

You will appear to go about your life as usual today. But you should know that you will actually be moving in a specially designed house of mirrors. Having been built by the Master himself, this is of course no ordinary carnival sideshow. Yet all the rules of reflection that you are familiar with will apply and will be the basis of everything you experience today.

What makes this house of mirrors different from one you may have seen at a county fair or a carnival is degree only. Here, everything about you will be reflected: your emotions, thoughts, words, behavior, as well as your bodily self-image. And, as in an ordinary house of mirrors, the image of each aspect of you will be repeated many times everywhere you look. Yet each time you see it, it will be exaggerated in some way as if by the curves of the mirrors into which you look.

In the usual house of mirrors, there is always a maze of mirrors through which you try to walk. If you become confused as to what you are seeing, you may very well bump into a surface, believing it to be a space. In today's game, the Master will not do anything to trick you. You will only be able to trick yourself. But if you remember that everything you see will be a literal reflection of some aspect of you, you will not bump into yourself.

The clear sign that you have forgotten what you are looking at is that you will feel angry. If there is any question about this, ask yourself if you are willing to stand by for a moment and review the rules of the game. If you feel a resistance to giving yourself this moment of rest, you have indeed become angry. Yet there is an easy way out. It involves only three rules. Apply them quickly and you will again be able to walk gently through this day.

Rule One: Do not fight yourself. This, of course, means not only accepting your behavior, your moods, your thoughts, and so forth, but also accepting everything about everyone you do not think is yourself. Remember, today you **are** in a house of mirrors, and to "accept" means merely to see.

Rule Two: Wait and calmly look around. To wait is to be patient, but patience does not mean to endure. Patience is the same as comfort and a free mind. "Looking around" releases the focus of your mind from whatever it has locked onto. Simply allow yourself to think what you think, see what you see, do what you do. Your attention will move easily about, and if you are consistent you will begin to feel a certain liking for everything.

Rule Three: Think gently and be content. Your mind can smile. Did you know that? Try it right now and you will see. Amusement without mockery is divine. Laugh softly at yourself. Notice how everyone does the best he can. There is no one undeserving of a gentle pat and the light touch of your love.

By the end of the day, if you have played this game even a little while, you will know what you have won. Your gift will be one of the golden rules of happiness: acceptance does not ignore what is negative and hurtful; it responds to it with healing. A call for help does not deserve your attack. And anyone who slights you is only telling you of his bitter need. Respond with your desire to gratify and comfort him, not your desire that he feel an even greater void.

When you recognize that what you do not

like is in you because you are choosing to hold it there, you will have released yourself. No longer are you a victim of the world you see. And in your freedom lies the freedom of every living thing.

Balls of Light

a light game

Light enters your perceptual world as God enters your thought. Yet God is no less God because He comes to your mind. It is inconceivable that He would not. If you should "donate" a part of your body to be used within another's body, yours would now appear to be lacking. Yet the way you will know that you are Light is by giving light away. The more you give it, the more brightly you will glow. It would be meaningless to suggest that your body should become one with all other bodies. Even if that were possible, it would mean your body's annihilation. Yet the light in you cannot help but join the light of everyone who has ever come, or is yet to come, forevermore. Today you will learn what is inside you by what comes from you. Therefore, give only love. You may believe that deep within you is darkness, yet there is only light.

GAME

Over your shoulder, the Master has placed a container that looks very much like a quiver or small golf bag. It contains balls of light each about the size of a snowball. There is an ample supply and every ball of light is within easy reach. When you take one out, it will appear to others that you are only scratching your neck or brushing something from your shoulder.

Whenever you toss up and catch one of these balls, it automatically doubles in size. Consequently, it is possible to make as large a ball of light as you desire by simply juggling it awhile. Since the light is pure, even one small ball is enough, yet please make the light as large as you think is needed to do the job you have in mind, and use as many of them as you believe will be helpful.

You may toss a ball of light at anyone or thing you wish. If it is very large, you may send it with both hands as you would pass a basketball. Or you can throw it like a beachball or bounce it off your forehead like a soccer ball. You can drop-kick it or punt it. It is so light you can even blow it or flip it with your finger. So use any means of delivery you wish.

Once it arrives, it will surround and completely fill the person, animal, building, or whatever you have targeted and will cause it to shine and shine until all you can see will be lovely to look at, healed, and made so very happy.

Please observe this one rule: After you have finished, make for yourself an identical-sized ball, toss it above your head, and let it settle over you, around you, and throughout you until you too glow as happily as the person or thing you have just blessed.

If you wish to use the balls of light for your own physical healing, this procedure may prove helpful. First send the light to anyone, anywhere, whom you imagine having a similar difficulty. Then let the light represent your gift of forgiveness for anyone you may mistakenly think is deserving of punishment, however slight. And after you recognize the gentle joy you can feel on becoming completely harmless, let the ball of healing light touch and encompass your body and fill your heart and mind.

Toys

A REALITY GAME

If you had gone to bed very angry at someone, and, when you woke in the morning, you remembered a vivid dream in which this person had been injured, you would recognize that the accident in the dream represented a picture of your own angry thoughts. And if, the next day, you had a fantasy in which this person became ill, you would again recognize that the fantasy illness was yet another image of your own anger. However, if before the day ended, you received word that this person had been mugged, would you think that the mugging was like the dream-accident or the fantasy-illness? Or would you believe that your own angry feelings were entirely separate from the mind of the mugger?

If you recognized that they were not, would you also recognize that the victim's mind was not separate from the mugger's and the mugger's not separate from his own conscious choice to assault those more helpless than himself? And if the thoughts of everyone who was aware of the mugging were equally a part of what happened, who, then, was to blame?

Responsibility and guilt are not the same. To the ego, there is fault in everything that happens, and so nothing occurs in which someone is not guilty. The ego's solution to this unhappy interpretation is to try to narrowly confine the guilt. That is why its first response to any problem is to identify the ones who are "responsible" and thereby lessen the blame on itself. But in so doing, it also limits your recognition of actual responsibility and your potential to be of help.

If the mugging had taken place only in your dream or in your fantasy, and you had instead received word of this person's illness, you might have been tempted to feel guilty. Perhaps you would believe there was a greater possibility that your angry wishes could have more to do with his illness than with an act of violence. Yet illness **is** an act of violence, and to picture someone as a victim of disease is to decline to offer him your gift of healing. Would it not be better, since your ego cannot decide what effect your thoughts do have on others, to assume complete responsibility for everything and guilt for nothing? Now, at least, you have placed yourself in a position to help. Love does not stand by, a helpless victim of either violence or guilt. Love is, not in this world but throughout this world.

It is hoped that in your play today you will see more clearly the difference between responsibility and guilt, for this will indeed make you very glad. The guilty see themselves helpless because the damage has been done and the cause has been labeled and dissociated. He who thinks he is guilty believes he is a victim of himself. Now he can only hope he will somehow become a victim of love. Awaiting only your welcome, not your submission, Love stands forever with you. To assume full responsibility is to renounce guilt as useless. If you are responsible for how you see the world, you are also completely free to see it differently. Choose, then, to play this little game of freedom.

GAME

Perhaps, when you were a child, you played a game similar in form to today's game. One day you became angry at someone, and you set out your toy figures in front of you. As you moved the toy people around like actors in a play, each figure became associated with a different thought in your conflicted mind, and you made a script in which the one you disliked was punished and taken from your sight.

When the game was done and the toys were put away, perhaps you were surprised when you reencountered the person you disliked to find that he had not been "taught a lesson" at all. You knew that change was needed, but, being a child, you did not yet know that games of anger and guilt solve nothing.

Today you will play a game that can work and therefore be truly enjoyable. Everyone you encounter today will be a toy, because, although each will appear quite lifelike, the Master has brought out his set of robots for you to play with. He has programmed them to endlessly amuse and comfort you, and, being perfectly turned to your thought waves, they know just how to respond to your every wish. Nothing is required of you because all they will do will be automatic. Your only part is to remember that because the robots are tuned to the vibrations of your mind, you will confuse them about their function if you allow your thoughts to become conflicted.

A conflicted mind sends out dual signals, and this will cause the robots to act in con-tradictory ways. If any robot you encounter today begins to misbehave, simply forgive him, and he will immediately be restored to his programmed purpose of making you happy. Whatever you do, do not begin thinking that you are to blame for his erratic behavior. Blame is a form of attack, and self-attack is highly conflicted. The mind seeks both its own advantage and its own punishment. Likewise, to blame the robot would be a mistake because it would be a wish to be left alone. There is no comfort in a wish for loneliness.

The solution to self-blame is not to blame another. Only forgiveness answers blame. To forgive is to let go. To let go is to forget. The power of your mind to forget is largely untapped. Forget to judge, even for an instant, and your mind becomes unified and pleased. Now all the Master's robots will be receiving an unequivocal signal.

Let us look for a moment at the signs that will appear around you, should you become conflicted today. Conflict is the wish for opposing realities. Although more than one thing is wanted, each is not sought after at the same instant. If your mind is having a temper tantrum, it will pursue one thing and then another. Each thing is sought only for the purpose of discovering what there is in it that you do not like. In this state, your mind does not know happiness and so it does not know what it likes, only what it hates, and its list of hates is very long.

It should be remembered that temper tantrums come in all speeds. You can turn slowly from one thing to another or very quickly. But slowness alone never indicates that the mind is more peaceful.

Today, the Master's robots will show you quite clearly what you are turning to now. Each robot will represent one of your thoughts just as each toy figure did when you were a child. The robot will look the way you request, act in the manner you order, and speak only the words you want to hear. Do not be confused by the fact that you do not like what you see and hear. You are seeing and hearing it because you do not like it. Remember that you like nothing, yet turn to everything, when you are conflicted. Forgiveness is your easy way out, and the only one that will work. Stop seeking and allow yourself to have. Do not want, simply be. Release your mind from multiple goals, and it will, entirely on its own, return to a single goal of enjoying deeply all its en-counters. You will know that this has hap-pened today when none of the Master's robots is distressed, in pain, or lacking for anything at all. It is their joy to serve you. They want nothing more than this. They know how holy a child of God you are.

Look the Tiger
In the Eye

AN OBSERVATION GAME

GAME

Perhaps you have heard children say that if you stare a charging tiger fearlessly in the eye, he will stop and back away. The governing word here is "fearlessly" and not "stare." Power lies in the release from fear, not in the attempt to provoke it. In the recognition of existing strength is calmness. One cannot look calmly at that which approaches and not be certain of the outcome. Calmness is trust based on reality.

Today's meditation is very simple. Whenever you feel distress, no matter what its form or degree, look at it calmly, steadily. Allow it to approach. Allow it to enter. Simply be still and smile on it awhile.

Casting Director

A PRAYER GAME

Of all the diverse and conflicting interpretations of what motivates your enemy that your past experiences might give rise to, and of an equal number read into your enemy's behavior by another observer, and still again of as many by another onlooker, and on and on, there is only one interpretation of this motivation that will accurately reflect the contents of his heart. All else will be merely someone's projected "lesson" from the past. Your experience must tell you of your experiences. The present communicates itself.

The only motive worth looking for in your enemy's actions is the one that will allow you to respond to him with healing and love. Does he truly ask anything else from you? If he says, "Attack me and make me whole," it is his wholeness he begs you to see, and he is merely mistaken in the means. If he asks you to attack yourself so that he may feel a sense of gain through your comparative loss, it is still in the means and not in the end he seeks that his mistake lies.

Do not inform him of his error and thereby add to his belief that he is not complete. Join with his wholeness and let your mind see nothing else. Your spiritual vision will inform him of itself. This instant he has everything he needs. Look gently on this happy fact until you see that it must apply equally to you.

GAME

Enemies are never new. They are old responses, not old relationships. The one you have chosen to play that role need only be recast into a gentler one.

If anyone becomes your enemy today, if even for a moment you believe that someone's interests and yours conflict, immediately rewrite the script of the encounter to serve a different purpose. Instead of casting this one as a depriver, rewrite the effect on you of his words and acts.

What, then, is the role of your enemy? Is he there to take from you or to give? He protects your mind by telling you when you are taking from yourself. And the way he appears to take from you is the very way you have chosen to deprive yourself. Give him what he asks of you and you will receive the same. Do not refuse him and make of him a thief.

But be certain not to misunderstand his request. Become him for just a moment in

your mind. Say his words and do his deeds
and know what he is truly asking of you in his
heart. He asks you to see what you would
want him to see in you. Nothing more than
this. He asks you to hear in his words the
gentle interpretation you would wish your
words be given.

From Another Planet

A REVIEW GAME

This game is designed to give you still another way to see the people you "know" without distortion from the past. Another's history will tell you nothing about how he is now. How he is now must be seen now, and recalling to mind how he was can only influence you to repeat an old reaction to an old interpretation. Resentments and grievances cry out for payment in kind or at least for secret rejoicing over another's loss. None of this adds any meaning to your life. Forget everything you "know" and remember what a pleasure love is. **It is more honest to be happy than to be right.**

GAME

Your planet recently established contact with another planet called "Earth." Everyone who has visited reports it is very beautiful and that the people of Earth are quite friendly when given half a chance. Last week your government called you in and asked if you would be interested in participating in an exchange program that had just been set up. You said that you certainly would be, and now

you are about to make your first exchange
visit.

The way the exchange is made is that two
people, one on each planet, agree to leave
their bodies right where they are and enter the
other person's body on its own planet. In this
way, no onlooker need be surprised by a
sudden switching of bodies, and no period of
adjustment to the new atmospheric conditions
is required.

The exchange of inner selves takes only
two seconds. And now you are blinking your
eyes and looking around for the first time at
Earth. You know nothing about the past of the
people you are with and nothing about the
quality of the relationships the body you are
now in has had with them. Before the exchange, you agreed to a completely clean
memory so that your attitude would not be
distorted by a single loveless thought. Now
you are free to do nothing but extend
goodwill and to look about at an entirely new
world.

Keyholes

A REALITY GAME

Today's game recognizes that the first step must be taken first. You must start with what you do see, and see it more honestly before you will be in a position to see what is at present invisible. Since another child of God is frequently viewed as a body that is different in all respects from the body of the observer, it is on this level that equality must first be sensed. For within equality is all loneliness and bitterness banished. To accomplish this, what is not different from you must be acknowledged. This is the coming of light. How, then, do you see what is exactly like you, right where all appears to be different? You can only begin. Seeing begins with the wish to see. As the wish deepens into will, so seeing deepens into vision. Say then, "Let me pause a moment and sense my yearning to know no one as a stranger. And let me begin with the one who is before me now."

GAME

You may be accustomed to thinking of bodies as opaque objects moving in clear space; yet the reverse is actually true. Space cannot be seen through because spiritual light does not pass through space. Bodies are really like keyholes, the old-fashioned kind that allowed a peek or like the more recent peepholes used in front doors. Seen accurately, bodies permit a full view of the real world. It is space, distance, a sense of separation, that blocks your view of reality, and not bodies. Bodies now symbolize your belief that distance exists. Yet it is possible to view bodies in such a way that you will recognize distance as the illusion. To allow you to do this with complete ease, the Master has designed for you a unique kind of eye wear. It is similar to glasses and yet is as inconspicuous as contacts. It is actually an energy field held in suspension and shaped for an exact wraparound fit over your eyes. There is now a microscopic skin pouch just beside the right corner of your right eye. Whenever you wish the "glasses" in place, touch that general area lightly two times and the "glasses" will instantly expand across your entire field of vision. If you are wearing ordinary glasses, these need not be removed.

With the energy-field "glasses" in place, the space between you and each body you see is automatically filled with something far more substantial than you are in a habit of thinking bodies to be. Only one thing fits this description, of course, and that is love. For the purposes of this game, love can be thought of as honor and appreciation and as thanks. Your "glasses" will send out a flood of honor and gratitude toward any body you see or think of and this will cause a reversal of your perceptual field. What you see will appear, at first, to be something like diamonds placed on lovely dark velvet or like campfires against a cool summer's night. The bodies will be where you can see, and as you look at them more and more gratefully, these points of light will appear to expand and join with each other and with you. This latter appearance will not be a deception.

Therefore, whenever your "glasses" are in place and you see a body, kindly think thoughts similar to these: "There goes the moving focal point of the entire universe. I will honor it. There is a mirror which, if I like, can be held up to the Heart of God. I am thankful for such an opportunity. There is the one thing within my world of limitations that can send forth a limitless blessing. I am glad it is near. There is the first place I will see my Savior. Do I not owe it respect?"

Then wait an instant for your world of images to stand upright in the light. Space will become love, and bodies will become the fountains through which the love spills.

Seen in this way, bodies are what is not separate from you. Space is only the belief that they are. Bodies are the places where you have yet to discover yourself. Distance is what is not there. Distance is a mirage placed between parts of your heart, yet a mirage cannot truly divide. Bodies mark the spots where you are connected.

When distance becomes great enough, it is referred to as "time." Time is "great" distance. A body appears separate from you only because you see in it your past. Be quiet awhile and let this perception reverse. Free all bodies from thoughts of what you used to be. Remember nothing about yourself, and bodies will become a welcome opening into now.

Allow your heart to move quickly across the time that divides you and another. Stand where another stands, breathe as he breathes, yearn for understanding as he yearns. See no differences between you and him, for differences are hate and hate makes space seem real. Hate is the wish for space between you and another. This day do you choose love in place of distance, honor in place of suspicion and thanks that this body, every body, has given you so accessible an opportunity to see God.

Three-Room House

A PRAYER GAME

GAME

Today's prayer game asks you to think of your mind as a house containing three rooms: the worldly room, the room of Light, and the Place of God. The house is bigger than any universe, and the walls of the rooms are as thin and as yielding as air. In the first room, by far the smallest, is the world of time and perception: strange images of all sorts; events that are senseless and cruel; loneliness, pain, and lack of communication; and all things running down to death. Here, anything that seems to shine, shines for a moment only and then is extinguished.

In the second room is only light. The song of heaven is heard throughout this one eternal day. No one can wear out his welcome, and wherever he turns is joy and endless peace.

The third room is really not a room at all, for it has no boundaries of any kind. Here is the Place of God. It actually surrounds and underlies everything, although, from within the sense of time and distance still inherent in the first two rooms, it appears to be a place to which one journeys. No words can describe the beauty and rapture of the Place of God.

Words were made as evidence of inequality, but all is One in God.

There should be no sense of urgency accompanying your play periods today. Two or three periods will be all you need to receive the rewards of the game. Begin in the first room of your mind and simply look about at what there is to see. As your attention rests on each thing, present or thought of, say to yourself, "There must be more to life than this." This statement is not meant to be one of denouncement, but one of realization. There **must** be more to life than just this.

Now you are ready to move into the second room. This will be the only other room you will attempt to enter today, because God is already with you, and to strive to enter Him is to misunderstand where He is. Remember that all you need to do to enter the second room is to pass through a wall of air. Picture yourself moving toward this wall and stopping just in front of it. Behind you now are all the old images of the first room. Before you is unending brillance extending in all directions. You lean your face into the wall of air and feel a slight pressure, almost like the skin of a bubble. This sensation is actually an illusion similar to one created by taking your hand out of ice water and putting it into water of room temperature. For just a moment, the room-temperature water will seem quite hot in comparison. Similarly, the wall of air before you is really the end of pressure. All the pressure is where you now stand, and on the other side is freedom unlike anything in this world.

Now you move forward and begin passing through the wall of air. The sensation is like rising to the surface of a lake or leaving the pressurized cabin of a plane. Feel the wall of pressure yield around you, and pass by you, as you enter the room of Light. Now all you can see is beauty. Love shines far more brightly and harmlessly than a thousand suns. As you look down at yourself, you see that you, too, have become a body of light as bright and undelineated as the boundless light that now surrounds you. You look back, and the first room has been shined away. You think, "I am the light, and I am in the light. The light is all I see, and everywhere it shines, I shine with it, forever and forevermore." And then your mind becomes quiet, as quiet as living light.

Brain Cells

A REVIEW GAME

Of all the true laws of cause and effect, perhaps the easiest to recognize is the law that you must receive what you give, you must learn what you teach. Anyone who has made a loving attempt to apply this idea to a relationship, even if only for a few moments, has felt the immediate delight of its effects. Today's game will give you a way to visualize this application.

GAME

Using advanced biofeedback technology, the Master has created a unique type of life-size doll. It is somewhat like the kind you can blow up and set in the front seat of your car so other drivers will not think you are alone (a typical ego solution). However, the Master's doll is far more lifelike and includes special electrodes that are attached to the cells of your brain. (For the purposes of this game only, please think of your brain as the source of your mind.) Whatever emotion or thought you express to the doll will feed directly back into your brain, and you will immediately have whatever you have given.

So foresightful is the Master that he has substituted one of these dolls for each of the people you were to encounter today. This includes even those your eyes "happen" to light on, as well as your old friends and acquaintances. Each time you see someone, it will be as if you are looking directly at one of your brain cells, and whatever you teach that cell, you will be teaching yourself. Whatever position you put someone else in, you will feel so placed.

Today, if you think to anyone, "You are different and separate from me," the lesson you will learn is that **you** are cut off and alone. However, if you quickly change that thought to, "We walk together, you and I," then the doll will transfer to your brain the lesson that you are fully joined and deeply meaningful to every living thing. Seek to make happy, and you will be happy. But seek to teach guilt, and you will feel attacked.

There is no limit to how much you can give yourself today, nor to all the deeply satisfying qualities you can extend directly to yourself. Perhaps one caution would be helpful. Trying to "please" another—trying to be popular or to be liked—is not an act of love, although your ego may attempt to so disguise it. The reason it is not is that this attitude assigns a role to the one to whom it is expressed and thereby makes a demand of him that threatens you with irritation should he not respond in a way you think fair. Therefore, give your gifts of love without expecting anything from the ones you serve, and your day will abound in gifts.

Personal Manager

A LIFE GAME

This is the only game in this book called a "life game." It is named that because there will never come a time when it will not increase your happiness to play it.

GAME

Knowing you well, the Master has suggested that you engage the services of a personal manager. You already know His name; that is, you already have some way of identifying His voice. It may be Jesus, God, Mary, Guide, your "deeper self," your inner knowing, your sanity, your peace, or any of a thousand other names or terms, or you may prefer no name, simply stillness. The point is that even though you recognize He is your friend, you may not be availing yourself of everything He has to offer you.

Please, in perfect safety and in well-deserved confidence, turn over to Him everything you now think of as yours. For example: your house, your money, your children, your friends, your career. Do not exclude anything: clothes, health, leisure, your secret moments, your private prides, your every idle thought. Remember, you can dismiss Him instantly and at any time. His help will never be forced on you. And although it will be very sad, you probably will dismiss Him many times before you recognize that your confidence in Him is well placed.

This quiet and very comfortable Friend, with all His managerial skills, knowing your needs and those of every other living thing, now walks with you wherever you may go. He will not desert you, even in your sleep. To avail yourself of His certain wisdom, ask of Him whatever questions you have. But do not entreat Him, for that will never be necessary.

Now the questions of whom should you help with your money, to whom should you open your home, where should you go and when, will not longer be judgments you need to make by yourself. You have no career but the one He provides you moment by moment; no other family but His whole creation; no time to kill, only His joy to live. And the satisfaction you have long hoped for will come from following His guidance and not from defending your specialness or standing, which never were able to quench the longing you have had to do and be good in His Name and Yours.

Any decisions you find yourself attempting to make by yourself, gladly, and with a little sigh of relief, turn immediately over to Him. Simply say, "**You decide.** I certainly have no way of knowing the full consequences of the least of my decisions or idle wishes." And that will be enough. Know now that it is taken care of. And walk again in peace.

Eraser

A REVIEW GAME

Today's game brings together several forms of play. It is meant to repeat a joy felt before and to offer you an example of how you can use everything in this book in any way you wish. It is especially designed to allow you to let go of painful memories and old scenes of misery, and yet it can also be played with the present moment or with moments believed to be on their way.

GAME

The three areas where you look most often for your experiences are in the words you think and hear, the images you see, and the sensations and emotions you feel. Even within the latter two areas, your mind is quick to name and describe. Today you will attempt to erase all the unnecessary intermediaries between you and what you experience. You will seek to live life directly.

First, practice identifying these three areas. As you think back on some experience, notice that you hear thoughts as words, you see objects and events as pictures, and you feel a different sensation in reaction to each of these.

Now look back again at this experience. Replace every word you think with the single word **love.** Use only this word for each word you recall that someone said to you, and only this for every new word your mind attempts to put in place of what you answered back. Any word remembered, thought of, or mentally spoken as a concept or idea, any word at all, replace now with the single word **love.**

Go back once more. Review the many pictures in your mind. Faces. Things moving and still. Half images and shadows. Whatever you see, replace now with one image only: **light.** Let this picture of light shine away the dark lines of delineation. Shadows are needed to make a separate picture, and instead of shadows you will see only endless light.

Now return one time more. Recall each feeling as it came. Remember every mood. Also be aware of your present reactions. And each time you focus on a feeling, however vague or sharp it is, replace it with the one feeling of **peace.** Be still and calm and rest awhile in gentleness.

Remembered in this way, this one event from the past will become a source of present assurance. Nothing about it will remain to confuse you because your purpose for recalling it will have changed completely. And should you forget your new goal and instead remember or anticipate anything for purposes of guilt or martyrdom, hold up again a single happy lesson in your mind. If some dark image of judgment is expected or recalled, see only light. If you hear a thought of attack, hear only love. And should a feeling of conflict arise in your mind, feel only peace.

Now, may peace, light, and love be yours.
Today and in the days to come.
And in all the days remembered,
may a single thought of rest
bless and comfort your mind.

EPILOGUE

Here are a few final suggestions, which, if you will follow them, will show you that this book has not presented you with just one more impossible dream. Certainly you have had ample proof that the world is full of "ways" that lead nowhere. Likewise, there are many forms of the one way that leads to certainty. The distinction between these two sets of ways is clear. One states, "The kingdom of God is within you." The other always counsels some form of external search.

But knowing that is not enough. If your resolve is weak, the results will be disappointing. Far more than knowing the way is needed. It must be followed or else nothing has really changed. Here then are some general rules of how to effectively implement the ideas presented in this book.

Begin your day by setting sharply in your mind your purpose for living. This cannot be overemphasized because a purposeless day, a day in which you wait for something to happen to you and then look back and ask yourself what it meant, has no chance of succeeding on any level.

Only an instant or two is needed, although more can be effectively used. Duration is not the goal; clarity is. It is good if this quiet time comes just after you wake, but if, because of your situation, that is not feasible, then give yourself this moment's headstart as soon as is practical.

A second general rule is to not fear starting your day over whenever you find you have lost your way. Once again, only a moment can be sufficient. Remind yourself of what your purpose is and Who is there to take your hand. Ask for His help and then continue on in gentle contentment.

The third rule follows from the first two. Before you sleep, release yourself from any burdens you carry. Let all awareness settle out of your mind, and thank Love for Its gifts, which are eternal. Remember that your dreams do not have to be conceded to your ego. Pause a moment before you lie down, and see clearly the mental tone you wish to carry through the night. If you wake during the night and find you do not like how you feel, try again for dreams of forgiveness and of love. Remember here, as during the day, a little gain is preferable to none at all.

If you sincerely want to walk in peace and know the presence of Love, then no matter what the approach you use, it will succeed to some degree, and you will be instructed quite

specifically as to how to improve on the part
you will be asked to play in bringing rest to
the world. Therefore, apply all that you know
to this instant. It does not matter what you do
not know. And each time you forget, try
again. This simple and direct approach will
take you much further than you ever dreamed
possible.

Arise With Me

O You who came in winter and who left
Among the lilies, stay with me and fill
My eyes with glory, and my heart with love
That smiles forever on the world You saw,
And that You loved as You would have me love.
For with this vision I will look on You,
And recognize my Savior in all things
I did not understand. Now is the world
Reborn in me because I share Your Love.
Now in my healed and holy mind there dawns
The memory of God. And now I rise
To Him in all the loveliness I knew
When I was first created one with You.